AF256907

This Book Belongs To:

____

BY

Home Planners And Journals

To help you organize your life

This book is copyright protected. Reproducing this book is prohibited and not allowed without the permission of the author. All rights reserved.

www.ingramcontent.com/pod-product-compliance
Lightning Source LLC
Chambersburg PA
CBHW050948050726
47592CB00007B/2482
* 9 7 8 1 7 9 7 6 6 5 8 4 9 *